IMPLEMENTING

Nursing's Report Card

A Study of RN Staffing, Length of Stay and Patient Outcomes

AMERICAN NURSES
ASSOCIATION

This study was conducted by the American Nurses Association in conjunction with NETWORK, Inc., a hospital and health care consulting firm. The primary research team at NETWORK, Inc., consisted of Robert A. Knauf, Leo K. Lichstig, PhD, Robin Rison-McCoy, RN, Andrew D. Singer, and Lynn Marie Wozniak, ART. For more information on the study, please contact the researchers at (800) 523-1394.

Library of Congress Cataloging-in-Publication Data

Implementing nursing's report card : a study of RN staffing, length of
  stay, and patient outcomes / American Nurses Association.
        p.   cm.
    Includes bibliographical references.
    ISBN 1-55810-134-9 (pbk.)
      1. Nurses—Supply and demand—United States.   2. Nursing services—
Standards—United States.   3. Hospital utilization—Length of stay—
United States.   4. Outcome assessment (Medical care).   5. Hospital
care—United States—Evaluation.   I. American Nurses' Association.
    [DNLM: 1. Nursing Care—standards.   2. Personnel Staffing and
Scheduling.   3. Outcome Assessment (Health Care)   4. Quality
Assurance, Health Care—organization & administration.   WY 100 I344 1997]
RT86.73.I48   1997
362.1'73'02373—dc21
DNLM/DLC
for Library of Congress   97-9524
                                                                                     CIP

Published by
American Nurses Publishing
600 Maryland Ave., SW
Suite 100 West
Washington, DC 20024-2571

Table of Contents

Results 23

Discussion 31

Tables

Executive Summary

Background

The American Nurses Association (ANA) is concerned both with the impact of nursing care on patient outcomes and the professional well-being of nurses. To affirm nursing's role in emerging health care systems and to advance knowledge in these areas, ANA commissioned and adopted a prototype for nursing report cards to measure nursing's impact on selected patient outcomes. This study uses data from 1992 and 1994 in three states—California, Massachusetts, and New York—to accomplish two primary goals:

- to statistically test the relationships between nurse staffing and specific patient outcome indicators, and
- to assess the feasibility of capturing the information necessary to develop specific nurse staffing and outcome measures for hospitals with acceptable degrees of reliability and validity.

Methodology

The methodology used in this study was designed to:

- quantify nurse staffing at the sample hospitals,
- quantify patient incidents and lengths of stay at the same hospitals; and,
- measure the relationship between these sets of variables.

Patient incidents studied include:

- Pressure Ulcers
- Pneumonia (not community acquired)

- Urinary Tract Infections
- Postoperative Infections

To control intervening variables in the relation of staffing and patient incidents, case-mix was measured as well as teaching status and setting (e.g., urban vs. rural).

- Hospitals were categorized as medical school affiliate, other teaching, and non-teaching.
- Three categories for settings were used--large urban, urban, and rural.
- The nurse staffing variables examined in this study included: 1) total nursing hours per Nursing Intensity Weight and 2) RN hours as a percentage of all nursing hours.

The primary variable thought to cause variation in patient incidents is the case-mix of patients treated at the hospitals being studied. To adjust for case-mix, Nursing Intensity Weights (NIW) developed by the New York State Nurses Association under a contract with the New York State Department of Health were employed. The NIW can be used to allocate hospitals' nursing costs to their patients in order to develop diagnosis related group (DRG) case-mix weights for case payments. The most recent set of NIWs were used to weight patient days in investigating nurse staffing.

The application of the NIWs to the three 1994 state data sets used in this study showed a highly significant direct correlation between average NIWs per day and average nursing hours and registered nursing hours per day for each of the three states.

Results

Acuity, staffing levels and skill mix are:

- greater in hospitals with high degrees of teaching and lowest degree of urbanity (i.e., those in rural settings);
- evenly distributed across geographic settings within each state, except for New York City; and,
- New York City metropolitan statistical area staffing levels were significantly lower in terms of nursing hours per patient day than in upstate New York.

All three states from 1992 to 1994 show:

- substantial increases in nurse staffing per patient day;
- modest increases in RN skill mix; and
- modest increases in case-mix acuity.

Staffing and patient incidents include:

- New York and California
  —Statistically significant *inverse* relationships for all four incidents in 1992 and 1994 (for example, as RN staffing increases, the number of pressure ulcers decreases).
  —Statistically significant *inverse* relationships for staffing and length of stay for 1992 and 1994 (e.g., increased staffing is associated with decreased length of stay);

- Massachusetts
  —Statistically significant **inverse** relationships for staffing and length of stay for 1992 and 1994;
  —In 1992, only pressure ulcers were statistically significant and inversely related; and,
  —In 1994, only pneumonia was statistically significant and inversely related.

Several states already mandate the collection of: 1) hospital uniform cost reports, which can be used to compute nurse staffing structural variables; and, 2) patient discharge abstracts, which can be used to cull complication rates and relative lengths of stay. Furthermore, some states mandate that cost reports include nurse staffing information. Patient data in these three states came from discharge abstract data including, at a minimum, the Uniform Hospital Discharge Data Set (UHDDS). The patient data from all three states were grouped into All Payor version 12 Diagnosis Related Groups, mapping ICD-9 CM codes adjusted for coding changes over the years.

California, Massachusetts, and New York were selected for this study because:

- Data from these states are publicly available at a reasonable cost;
- The data are reasonably current;
- The states contain a sizable percentage of the nation's hospitals, patients, and nurses; and,
- California, Massachusetts, and New York are representative of regional differences in patient care.

For the four patient incidents and the length of stay index, regressions were performed individually for New York, California, and Massachusetts for 1992 and 1994, respectively, to test their relationship with the independent variables: teaching status, setting, total nursing hours per NIW, and registered nurse percentage of total nursing hours.

Limitations

Limitations to this study include:

- It is an unspecified model;
- Numerous factors in a hospital's environment other than case mix, teaching mission and setting may impact the incidence of the selected complications and patients' length of stay.

Chief difficulties in conducting this study include:

- Data quality and timeliness problems encountered with state data sets; and
- Reporting of complicating secondary diagnoses, which were significantly lacking for Massachusetts and may have been to a lesser extent in the other states as well.

Conclusions

The project successfully achieved the following goals and objectives:

- Numerous indicators for the *Nursing Care Report Card for Acute Care* were measured in 502 total hospitals in California, Massachusetts, and New York:

California	295 Hospitals
Massachusetts	76 Hospitals
New York	131 Hospitals
	502 Total Hospitals

- Shorter lengths of stay were found to be strongly related to higher nurse staffing per acuity-adjusted day;
- Patient morbidity indicators for preventable conditions—pressure ulcers, pneumonia, postoperative infections, and urinary tract infections—were found to be statistically significantly inversely related to registered nurse skill mix, and, to a lesser extent, nurse staffing per acuity-adjusted day; and,
- Nursing Intensity Weights by DRG were found to be statistically significantly directly related to differences in nurse staffing ratios per patient day in all three states.

Introduction

The science and art of nursing are at a crossroads today between the tremendous increase in demand for health care services experienced during the '60s, '70s and '80s and the national movement by government, employers and insurers to economize the provision of care. The American Nurses Association (ANA), as the spokesperson for the profession of nursing, is concerned with both the impact of nursing care on patient outcomes and with the economic position of nurses. To advance the state of knowledge in these areas, the ANA commissioned and adopted a theoretical prototype for nursing report cards[1] which proposed twenty-one measurable indicators of nursing structure, process and outcome for acute care settings. The ability to quantify—from a cost/benefit perspective—the practice of nursing and its impact on patient care outcomes and costs may well be a prerequisite for the health of the profession as it moves into the twenty-first century.

This present study is a pilot project to determine the practicality of monitoring several of the report card indicators mentioned above. It uses three state settings (California, New York and Massachusetts) for two years (1992, a year following the most recent nursing "shortage" in which demand for nursing ran quite high, and 1994, the most recent year of full data availability) to fulfill the study's two primary goals:

- to assess the feasibility of capturing the information necessary to develop specific nurse staffing and outcome measures for hospitals in those states with acceptable degrees of reliability and validity, and
- to statistically test the relationships between specific patient outcome indicators and nurse staffing.

The manner in which these dual purposes were accomplished is laid forth in the sections which follow: input state data sets, methodology, results and discussion.

---

[1] American Nurses Association. 1996. *Nursing Quality Indicators Definitions and Implications*. Washington, DC: Author.

Input State Data Sets

Several states mandate collection of both hospital uniform cost reports (which can be used to compute nurse staffing structural variables) and patient discharge abstracts (which can be used to cull adverse outcome rates and relative lengths of stay). Of these, California, Massachusetts and New York were selected because their data are publicly available for a reasonable cost; the data are reasonably current; the states contain a sizable percentage of the nation's hospitals, patients and nurses; they are representative of any differences in patient care which may be provided in the East compared with the West. In addition, these states are among those the research team had considerable experience working with, making them attractive for a pilot study.

Hospital Cost Reports

Uniform reporting of hospital nurse staffing and skill mix is not available nationally from either Medicare cost reports, voluntarily submitted American Hospital Association Annual Survey reports or any other source. However, approximately twenty states mandate reporting of hospital costs and statistics, including nurse staffing information. The three states selected herein were in part included due to the availability of such cost reports, as well as their size and geographic representativeness.

Hospital cost reports not only provide information about costs, but also about other factors involved in the operation of hospitals. State mandated cost reports usually include information on nursing hours by skill level, and sometimes by cost center. For the three states selected, the quality of data received was very uneven, especially nursing hours.

California: The Annual Hospital Disclosure Report was obtained for fiscal years 1992 and 1994 for all California acute hospital facilities. Data items obtained from these reports included, by cost center, total patient days, registered nurse (RN) hours, licensed vocational nurse (LVN) hours, and aides and orderlies. For 1994, seven hospitals did not submit cost reports, twenty six submitted but did not report nursing hours and eight reported unrealistic nursing hours (for 1992, twelve, twenty five and eleven, respectively).

Massachusetts: The 1992 and 1994 Hospital Statement for Reimbursement (RSC 403) was obtained for all acute care hospitals in Massachusetts. From these reports, total patient days, total full-time equivalents (FTEs) by cost center, and FTEs by nursing skill level (registered nurses; licensed practical nurses; and aides, orderlies and attendants) were collected. For 1994, eight hospitals did not submit cost reports, two submitted but did not report nursing hours and three reported unrealistic nursing hours (for 1992, four, sixteen and three).

New York: The 1992 and 1994 Institutional Cost Reports (ICRs) were used to obtain total patient days, total FTEs by cost center, and FTEs by nursing skill level (registered nurses, licensed practical nurses, and nursing assistants) for all acute care hospitals in New York State. For 1994, fifteen hospitals submitted no cost report, twenty-seven submitted but did not report nursing hours, and an additional twenty-one supplied unrealistic nursing hours (for 1992, twenty seven, thirty and eight).

Patient Level Data

While cost reports provide information about hospital cost structures and nurse staffing patterns, additional data are required to examine the outcomes of the care provided. Patient level data were collected to examine the case-mix of patients treated in the three states selected for this pilot study, and to measure selected outcomes of the care these patients received. All three states have statewide systems for collecting discharge abstract data including at least the Uniform Hospital Discharge Data Set (UHDDS).[2]

California: The California Office of Statewide Health Planning and Development (OSHPD) collects and maintains an annual file of case-mix data for every hospital in the state. For this study, the 155 byte Tape A format was obtained from OSHPD for 1992 and 1994. This format contains most data items in the UHDDS and are listed in Appendix A. Each year contained data for about 3.5 million discharges.

---

[2] U.S. National Committee on Vital and Health Statistics. 1985. *Uniform Hospital Discharge Data: Minimum Data Set.* Washington, DC: U.S. Government Printing Office.

TABLE 1   State Data Sources

State	Source	1994 Total Acute Hospitals	1994 Hospitals Used*	
California	Office of Statewide Health Planning and Development	462	295	(63.9%)
Massachusetts	Massachusetts Rate Setting Commission	92	76	(82.6%)
New York	Statewide Planning and Research Cooperative System	229	131	(57.2%)

*Unidentifiable hospitals and hospitals with fewer than two discharges per day were excluded, as well as hospitals with unusable data.

Massachusetts: The Commonwealth of Massachusetts Rate Setting Commission (RSC) collects and maintains annual files of case-mix and charge data for every hospital in the state. For this study, the Level One Case Mix file was obtained from the RSC for 1992 and 1994. The Level One data set includes all data items in the UHDDS except those that might be used to identify individual patients (e.g., exact dates of admission, discharge and birth) plus charge data by revenue center. The data items changed between 1992 and 1994, but the changes were in the level of detail of the revenue centers reported and did not impact this study. The data items provided are listed in Appendix B. Each year contained data for about 900,000 discharges.

New York: The Statewide Planning and Research Cooperative System (SPARCS) Bureau of the New York State Department of Health maintains annual files of case-mix and billing data for every hospital in the state. For this study, the Administratively Releasable file (Version 1) from SPARCS was used. This file contains all data items in the UHDDS except those that might be used to identify individual patients (e.g., exact dates of admission, discharge and birth). The items provided are listed in Appendix C. Each year contained information for about 2.5 million discharges.

The patient level data from all three states were grouped into All Payor version 12 Diagnosis Related Groups (DRGs), mapping ICD-9-CM codes as required to adjust for coding changes over the years. Table 1 summarizes the data sets.

Methodology

The methodology used in this study was designed to:

- quantify nurse staffing at the sample hospitals,
- quantify adverse outcomes and length of stay at the same hospitals, and
- measure the relationship between these sets of variables.

In order to link nursing structure and patient outcomes, intervening risk factors must be controlled for and measured. The primary such factor is the case-mix of patients treated at the hospitals being studied. Teaching hospitals, for example, have long been observed to have nurse staffing ratios, lengths of stay and mortality rates substantially higher than community hospitals, but these differences are, to a large extent, related to their more difficult mix of cases treated.

The relationship of nurse staffing to diagnostic case-mix and age was an early factor recognized in the development of DRGs (the most commonly used technique for case-mix measurement) in the early 1970s at Yale University. For this reason, nursing intensity weights were used to adjust the nurse staffing for nursing case-mix.

Factors affecting the measurement of adverse outcomes include differences in coding diagnoses in the different states. For example, states with all-payor DRG payment systems will likely have more secondary diagnoses coded than in states where financial incentives are not as strong. To adjust for such differences, outcome measures were never compared across states, but each hospital was measured against the averages for its own state. Thus, a hospital with an adverse outcome rate (case-mix adjusted) twice the state average would have an index value of 2.0; however, hospitals in two states with an index value of 2.0 may have different raw rates of that adverse outcome.

After the properly adjusted variables were computed for the hospitals in all three states, analysis focused on identifying whether the amount of nursing provided to patients had any impact on adverse outcome rates. For example, does more nursing result in fewer adverse outcomes? The rest of this section more fully describes the methods used.

Nurse Staffing Variables

Two nurse staffing variables were examined for this study:

- total nursing hours per Nursing Intensity Weight, and,
- RN hours as a percentage of all Nursing hours.

To obtain these values for each hospital in the three states, the hospital cost report data were manipulated and combined with the patient level data by performing the steps outlined below:

1. It was necessary to obtain the number of total nursing (RN, LVN, LPN and nursing assistant) hours and total RN hours on inpatient nursing units, excluding outpatient and ancillary service centers (e.g., operating rooms). This was readily available from the California hospitals because the Annual Disclosure Report requires this level of detailed reporting. However, while both New York and Massachusetts require hospitals to submit data regarding the number of hours worked by type of position and the number of hours worked by cost center, they instruct hospitals to report these numbers in separate schedules. Therefore, it was necessary for New York and Massachusetts, to allocate the total number of hours worked by RNs, LPNs and nursing assistants to the cost centers in which they worked. Because California hospitals report registered nurse hours and total nursing hours per cost center as a percentage of the total hours worked in each cost center they were used to determine appropriate allocation percentages among cost centers for the actual hours worked for each skill level.

   Not all New York State, California, and Massachusetts acute care hospitals were used in the study. Some hospitals from each state for each year had to be removed because they lacked believable information regarding patient days, hours by type of position, or hours by cost center; or the total hours by cost center varied by more than ten percent from the sum of hours by type of position.

   The allocation methodology consisted of two parts. First, for each ancillary cost center, registered nurse hours as a percentage of total hours were obtained for each of the California hospitals that submitted usable cost report data for the fiscal year 1992. The mean of these percentages was used as the standard registered nurse percent of total hours (including non-nursing personnel) for the corresponding ancillary cost center for New York and Massachusetts hospitals (See Table 2).

   The second part of the allocation methodology involved inpatient and ambulatory cost centers. For these cost centers, only those California hospitals that offered a particular inpatient or ambulatory service were used in calculating the mean percentage of total hours that were registered nurse hours and the percentage that were other nursing hours (See Table 2).

For the actual allocation of hospital hours, the number of hours per cost center was multiplied by the standard percentage of registered nurse hours obtained from the California hospital cost reports to yield an initial estimate of registered nurse hours per cost center. Next, this value was divided by the sum of the initial estimates of all cost centers to give the percent of hospital-wide registered nurse hours. Finally, this percentage was multiplied by the total number of registered nurse hours for each hospital to yield the final estimate of Registered Nurse hours for the cost center. The same allocation methodology was used to obtain the number of other nursing hours for each New York and Massachusetts hospital for which there were complete data.

Once the total number of RN and total nursing hours per cost center had been estimated, the values were summed across inpatient cost centers to obtain total inpatient RN hours per hospital and total inpatient all skill levels nursing hours per hospital.

2. The total number of patient days (obtained from the hospital cost reports) was divided into the inpatient total nursing hours per hospital (obtained from the above step) to determine the total nursing hours per day.

3. The patient level data sets were used to determine the total NIW value (see discussion below) for each hospital in each state for each year as described above. This was accomplished by multiplying the per diem NIW value for each DRG (See Appendix D) by the total number of inpatient days for the corresponding DRG and summing the resulting total DRG NIWs to obtain total NIWs per hospital.

4. The patient level data sets were used to obtain the total number of patient days reported on patient abstracts at each hospital. These values were divided into total NIWs per hospital to arrive at total hospital NIWs per day.

5. The total nursing hours per day were divided by total hospital NIWs per day to obtain RN hours per NIW and total nursing hours per NIW.

Nursing Intensity Weights

In order to recognize differences in patients' acuity of need for nursing care, the New York State Department of Health contracted with the New York State Nurses Association (NYSNA) to develop per diem Nursing Intensity Weights which could be used to allocate hospitals' nursing costs to their patients in order to develop DRG case-mix weights for case payments. These NIWs were first developed by a broadly representative special panel of NYSNA in 1985 and with nearly annual amendments and two complete updates (1989 and 1992) have been used to set payment rates for all inpatients (excluding Medicare) in New York State acute hospitals between 1985 and 1996.

New York State's use of these NIWs have been the only attempt to directly recognize nursing acuity within a reimbursement system in North America to date. Since nursing has never been a direct revenue (i.e., charging) center, its costs

TABLE 2   Nursing Percentage of Worked Hours by Direct Patient Care Cost Center

Cost Center	Registered Nurse	Other Nursing	Total Nursing
Adult Day Health Care	0.0%	22.0%	22.0%
Alternate Birthing	81.1%	0.2%	81.3%
Ambulatory Surgery	64.3%	8.9%	73.1%
Anesthesiology	3.2%	2.7%	5.9%
Blood Bank	1.8%	0.6%	2.4%
Burn Care	67.5%	10.1%	77.6%
Cardiac Cath	9.7%	0.4%	10.1%
Cardiology	2.9%	1.7%	4.7%
Coronary Care Unit	83.5%	2.4%	85.9%
Clinical Labs	0.7%	5.7%	6.4%
Clinics	14.6%	10.4%	25.0%
Computerized Tomography	0.8%	1.0%	1.8%
Definitive Obesrvation	62.6%	18.9%	81.5%
Drug Rehabilitation	33.1%	12.6%	45.7%
Drugs	1.0%	1.1%	2.1%
Durable Medical Equipment	0.0%	0.3%	0.3%
EEG	0.2%	0.1%	0.3%
EKG	0.3%	0.7%	1.0%
Electroconvulsive Therapy	72.5%	18.3%	90.8%
Electromyography	0.1%	0.2%	0.3%
Emergency Room	60.4%	9.4%	69.9%
GI Services	19.7%	4.6%	24.4%
Home Health	43.1%	20.1%	63.2%
Hospice	52.2%	16.4%	68.6%
Intermediate Care	19.1%	56.0%	75.1%
Inpatient Rehab	44.5%	37.3%	81.8%
Labor & Delivery	39.6%	3.8%	43.4%
Lithotripsy	3.2%	0.3%	3.6%
Medical Supplies	0.7%	9.7%	10.4%
Medical Surgical Acute	53.0%	34.5%	87.4%
Medical Surgical ICU	83.5%	2.7%	86.2%
Medical Transport Services	1.8%	0.5%	2.3%
MRI	0.6%	1.5%	2.2%
Neonatal Intensive Care	85.7%	1.6%	87.3%
Nuclear Medicine	1.0%	1.1%	2.0%
Nursery	75.7%	14.7%	90.4%

have been recovered through either flat per diem room and board charges or flat per diem allocations of room and board costs. Differences in patients' nursing needs, care and costs within medical-surgical obstetrics/gynecology and pediatrics are ignored by a flat per diem approach. Certainly the cost of nursing for a patient with stomach cancer recuperating from a major gastrointestinal surgery will differ from that of a patient undergoing non-malignant minor gynecological surgery. However, the amount of nursing costs per day in Medicare PPS rates will be the same for the non-intensive care days.

The NIW Panel's charge was to establish relative per diem weights for nursing acuity for each day of stay for a hypothetical "typical" patient in each DRG, guided by a comprehensive profile of statewide patients in that DRG (e.g., age, sex, payor, admission source and discharge status, and frequencies of specific principal and secondary diagnoses and procedure). A scenario fitting the data was then pro-

TABLE 2 Nursing Percentage of Worked Hours by Direct Patient Care Cost Center (Continued)

Cost Center	Registered Nurse	Other Nursing	Total Nursing
OB—Acute	66.6%	15.7%	82.3%
Observation Care	54.7%	6.1%	60.8%
Outpatient Drug Rehab	0.9%	0.4%	1.4%
Outpatient Hospice	1.1%	0.8%	2.0%
Organ Acquisition	0.1%	0.0%	0.1%
Occupational Therapy	0.6%	3.3%	3.9%
Other Outpatient	13.3%	5.1%	18.4%
Other Acute	35.7%	18.4%	54.1%
Other Ambulatory Services	0.0%	0.3%	0.3%
Other Daily Hospital Services	31.4%	30.0%	61.4%
Other ICU	75.9%	4.7%	80.6%
Other Physical Med	2.5%	0.9%	3.4%
Partial Hosp. Psych	21.9%	16.0%	37.9%
Pathology	0.0%	1.7%	1.8%
Peidatric Intensive Care	81.0%	2.8%	83.8%
Pediatrics Acute	71.2%	22.4%	93.5%
Psych Outpatient	0.8%	0.2%	1.0%
Psych Acute—Adult	39.0%	34.4%	73.4%
Psych Acute—PED	29.8%	45.6%	75.4%
Psych Emergency Room	16.0%	7.7%	23.7%
Psych Intensive Care	35.1%	48.0%	83.1%
Psych Long Term Care	25.0%	45.8%	70.8%
Psych Testing	0.0%	0.6%	0.6%
Physical Therapy	0.7%	11.3%	12.0%
Pulmonary Function	0.6%	0.4%	1.0%
Radiology—Diagnostic	0.5%	1.6%	2.0%
Ratiology—Therapeutic	1.3%	2.4%	3.8%
Renal Dialysis	6.1%	0.9%	7.0%
Residential Care	0.2%	0.6%	0.8%
Respiratory Therapy	1.0%	0.7%	1.8%
Skilled Nursing Care	20.0%	66.4%	86.5%
Speech Therapy	0.3%	0.1%	0.4%
Sub-Actue	21.5%	74.5%	96.0%
Surgery & Recovery	40.4%	10.3%	50.7%
Ultrasound	0.2%	1.1%	1.3%

posed by a clinical leader and discussed by the group who then individually assessed the hypothetical patient across six equally weighted dimensions of care using a one to five scale for each:

- Assessment
- Planning
- Physical Needs
- Medical Needs
- Socioemotional Support
- Teaching

Scores were combined and averaged across the panel using a modified Delphi process, such that absolute agreement was not called for but DRGs with significant divergences of scores were re-discussed and re-weighted. These subjectively de-

TABLE 3   Nursing Hours Per Day in Hospitals with High vs. Low NIWs Per Day

	California		New York		Massachusetts	
	Total Hrs/Day	*RN Hrs/Day*	*Total Hrs/Day*	*RN Hrs/Day*	*Total Hrs/Day*	*RN Hrs/Day*
Maximum hospital	17.0	12.0	13.4	9.8	15.6	13.2
Average of top 1/3 by NIW per day	8.7	6.5	9.2	5.7	10.2	7.4
Mean all hospitals	8.4	5.9	8.5	5.2	9.9	7.1
Average of bottom 1/3 by NIW per day	8.3	5.5	8.2	4.9	9.6	7.0
Minimum hospital	4.1	2.8	5.0	2.7	6.2	4.4
R-squared	21.7%	23.3%	27.4%	24.0%	12.2%	23.2%
Statistical significance	<.01	<.01	<.01	<.01	<.01	<.05

rived scores were then tested by applying them to patient specific data for a sample of one hundred hospitals and found, together with teaching status, to be statistically significant predictors of average cost per day differences in nursing costs across hospitals as provided by cost reports.[3]

For purposes of the current project, the most recent set of NIWs were used to weight patient days in investigating nurse staffing. The NIW one to five acuity scores were themselves weighted by the patient-to-nurse staffing ratio guideline used in developing the NIW scoring system.

The application of the NIWs to the three 1994 state data sets used in the current study showed a highly significant correlation between average NIWs per day (i.e., patient acuity as measured by DRGs) and average nursing hours and registered nursing hours per day for each of the three (See Table 3).

While certainly imperfect, DRGs and NIWs offer a reasonable, readily applicable and consistent alternative to not adjusting for case-mix in relating nurse staffing patterns to patient outcomes. The average per diem NIWs for each AP-12 DRG are listed in Appendix D. These NIWs were applied to the patient records of each hospital in the study to calculate an average daily acuity value for each hospital.

Adverse Outcomes

The following adverse outcomes were selected for investigation in this pilot study:

- Pressure ulcers
- Pneumonia
- Urinary tract infections
- Postoperative infections

Using the 1992 New York State discharge abstracts, more than 2700 diagnoses were analyzed. ICD-9-CM codes that appeared as secondary diagnoses more than 100 times in these discharge abstracts were reviewed and classified by a nurse and a clinical coding specialist on the research team into one of three categories:

[3] Ballard K.A., R.F. Gray, R.A. Knauf, and P. Uppal. 1993. Measuring Variations in Nursing Care per DRG. *Nursing Management*, 1993, 24 (4), 33–41.

1. LIKELY that it is an adverse outcome of the hospital stay;
2. UNLIKELY that it is an adverse outcome of the hospital stay;
3. NOT APPLICABLE.

In addition, the likely adverse outcomes were further classified as: Pressure Ulcers, Nosocomial (potentially postoperative) Infections, Pneumonia or Urinary Tract Infections.

A unique feature of the New York patient data is that all secondary diagnoses are flagged by the hospital medical record coders as having been present at admission or as developing after admission. For every secondary diagnosis, the percentage of times it developed after admission was used to help with assigning the likely/unlikely designations.

A diagnosis was designated as being "LIKELY" to have been a hospital adverse outcome if it was:

■ an acute short-term diagnosis that was flagged as occurring after admission in a high percentage of cases (>30%);
■ an iatrogenic or adverse outcome code (e.g., blood transfusion reaction, post-op infection code); or
■ a specific condition that since it was in a secondary diagnosis position indicated that it was not the reason for admission and therefore, not likely present at admission (i.e. gram negative or staph pneumonia, decubitus, pulmonary embolism, hypotension).

A diagnosis was designated as being "UNLIKELY" to have been a hospital adverse outcome if it was:

■ a chronic condition (i.e. diabetes, hypertension, CAD, COPD, CHF); or
■ a condition that was rarely flagged as happening after admission (e.g., malnutrition, adhesions).

Finally, a diagnosis was designated as "NOT APPLICABLE" if it was:

■ a code that was a supplementary explanation code (i.e. identifying the infecting organism);
■ a code that identified patient status (i.e., history of cancer, hip replacement status, etc.); or
■ a code that identified a neoplasm or other disease that could not be caused by hospitalization experiences.

Table 4 lists those diagnoses flagged as likely adverse outcomes. All secondary diagnoses for each patient record in the study were searched to identify any flagged diagnoses for each of the four adverse outcome categories. For example, a patient with a pneumonia code would be flagged for both the pneumonia category and the postoperative infection category if any procedure on their record was an operating room surgery.

Adverse outcome rates were calculated by DRG for each hospital and for each state as a whole within each of the two years. The postoperative infection rates were based on surgical discharges only. All other rates were based on all

TABLE 4   Diagnoses Used to Identify Adverse Outcomes
0 = Not an Adverse Outcome   1 = An Adverse Outcome

ICD-9-CM CODE	Diagnosis	Decubitus	Pneumonia	UTI	Post Op* Infection
00845	C. DIFFICILE ENTERITIS	0	0	0	1
00849	OTH BACTERIAL ENTERITIS	0	0	1	1
00861	ROTAVIRUS ENTERITIS	0	0	0	1
0380	STREPTOCOCCAL SEPTICEMIA	0	0	0	1
0381	STAPHYLOCOCC SEPTICEMIA	0	0	0	1
0383	ANAEROBIC SEPTICEMIA	0	0	0	1
03840	GRAM-NEG SEPTICEMIA NOS	0	0	0	1
03842	E COLI SEPTICEMIA	0	0	0	1
03843	PSEUDOMONAS SEPTICEMIA	0	0	0	1
03844	SERRATIA SEPTICEMIA	0	0	0	1
03849	OTH GRAM-NEG SEPTICEMIA	0	0	0	1
0479	VIRAL MENINGITIS NOS	0	0	0	1
0529	VARICELLA UNCOMPLICATED	0	0	0	1
0542	HERPETIC GINGIVOSTOMAT	0	0	0	1
05479	H SIMPLEX COMPLICAT NEC	0	0	0	1
0549	HERPES SIMPLEX NOS	0	0	0	1
0579	VIRAL EXANTHEMATA NOS	0	0	0	1
0779	VIRAL/CHLAM CONJUNCT DIS	0	0	0	1
1119	DERMATOMYCOSIS NOS	0	0	0	1
1120	THRUSH	0	0	0	1
1121	CANDIDAL VULVOVAGINITIS	0	0	0	1
1122	CANDIDIAS UROGENITAL NEC	0	0	0	1
1123	CUTANEOUS CANDIDIASIS	0	0	0	1
1124	CANDIDIASIS OF LUNG	0	0	0	1
1125	DISSEMINATED CANDIDIASIS	0	0	0	1
11284	ESOPHAGEAL CANDIDIASIS	0	0	0	1
11289	CANDIDIASIS SITE NEC	0	0	0	1
1129	CANDIDIASIS SITE NOS	0	0	0	1
1173	ASPERGILLOSIS	0	0	0	1
1175	CRYPTOCOCCOSIS	0	0	0	1
1179	MYCOSES NEC & NOS	0	0	0	1
13100	UROGENITAL TRICHOMON NOS	0	0	0	1
13101	TRICHOMONAL VAGINITIS	0	0	0	1
13109	UROGENITAL TRICHOMON NEC	0	0	0	1
1318	TRICHOMONIASIS NEC	0	0	0	1
1319	TRICHOMONIASIS NOS	0	0	0	1
1320	PEDICULUS CAPITIS	0	0	0	1
1322	PHTHIRUS PUBIS	0	0	0	1
1330	SCABIES	0	0	0	1
1363	PNEUMOCYSTOSIS	0	1	0	1
2870	ALLERGIC PURPURA	0	0	0	1
3229	MENINGITIS NOS	0	0	0	1
3239	ENCEPHALITIS NOS	0	0	0	1
4809	VIRAL PNEUMONIA NOS	0	1	0	1
481	PNEUMOCOCCAL PNEUMONIA	0	1	0	1
4820	K. PNEUMONIAE PNEUMONIA	0	1	0	1
4821	PSEUDOMONAL PNEUMONIA	0	1	0	1
4822	H.INFLUENZAE PNEUMONIA	0	1	0	1
48230	STREPTOCOC PNEUMONIA NOS	0	1	0	1
8239	STREPTOCOC PNEUMONIA NEC	0	1	0	1
4824	STAPHYLOCOCCAL PNEUMONIA	0	1	0	1
48282	E. COLI PNEUMONIA	0	1	0	1
48283	GRAM NEG PNEUMONIA NEC	0	1	0	1

TABLE 4 **Diagnoses Used to Identify Adverse Outcomes (Continued)**
0 = Not an Adverse Outcome   1 = An Adverse Outcome

ICD-9-CM CODE	Diagnosis	Decubitus	Pneumonia	UTI	Post Op* Infection
48289	BACTERIAL PNEUMONIA-NEC	0	1	0	1
4829	BACTERIAL PNEUMONIA NOS	0	1	0	1
4830	M.PNEUMONIAE PNEUMONIA	0	1	0	1
4841	PNEUM W CYTOMEG INCL DIS	0	1	0	1
4846	PNEUM IN ASPERGILLOSIS	0	1	0	1
485	BRONCHOPNEUMONIA ORG NOS	0	1	0	1
486	PNEUMONIA, ORGANISM NOS	0	1	0	1
4871	FLU W RESP MANIFEST NEC	0	0	0	1
490	BRONCHITIS NOS	0	0	0	1
5070	FOOD/VOMIT PNEUMONITIS	0	1	0	1
5078	SOLID/LIQ PNEUMONIT NEC	0	1	0	1
5100	EMPYEMA WITH FISTULA	0	0	0	1
5109	EMPYEMA W/O FISTULA	0	0	0	1
5111	BACT PLEUR/EFFUS NOT TB	0	0	0	1
5672	SUPPURAT PERITONITIS NEC	0	0	0	1
5678	PERITONITIS NEC	0	0	0	1
5679	PERITONITIS NOS	0	0	0	1
5731	HEPATITIS IN VIRAL DIS	0	0	0	1
5733	HEPATITIS NOS	0	0	0	1
58089	ACUTE NEPHRITIS NEC	0	0	0	1
5809	ACUTE NEPHRITIS NOS	0	0	0	1
5811	EPIMEMBRANOUS NEPHRITIS	0	0	0	1
5990	URIN TRACT INFECTION NOS	0	0	1	1
67002	MAJOR PUERP INF-DEL P/P	0	0	0	1
67004	MAJOR PUERP INF-POSTPART	0	0	0	1
68102	ONYCHIA OF FINGER	0	0	0	1
68111	ONYCHIA OF TOE	0	0	0	1
6821	CELLULITIS OF NECK	0	0	0	1
6822	CELLULITIS OF TRUNK	0	0	0	1
6823	CELLULITIS OF ARM	0	0	0	1
6824	CELLULITIS OF HAND	0	0	0	1
6825	CELLULITIS OF BUTTOCK	1	0	0	1
683	ACUTE LYMPHADENITIS	0	0	0	1
684	IMPETIGO	0	0	0	1
6851	PILONIDAL CYST W/O ABSC	0	0	0	1
6860	PYODERMA	0	0	0	1
6861	PYOGENIC GRANULOMA	0	0	0	1
6868	LOCAL SKIN INFECTION NEC	0	0	0	1
6869	LOCAL SKIN INFECTION NOS	0	0	0	1
690	ERYTHEMATOSQUAMOUS DERM	0	0	0	1
6918	OTHER ATOPIC DERMATITIS	0	0	0	1
6923	TOPICAL MED DERMATITIS	0	0	0	1
6924	CHEMICAL DERMATITIS NEC	0	0	0	1
69289	DERMATITIS NEC	0	0	0	1
6929	DERMATITIS NOS	0	0	0	1
6930	DRUG DERMATITIS NOS	0	0	0	1
6931	DERMAT D/T FOOD INGEST	0	0	0	1
6944	PEMPHIGUS	0	0	0	1
6945	PEMPHIGOID	0	0	0	1
6951	ERYTHEMA MULTIFORME	0	0	0	1
6953	ROSACEA	0	0	0	1
69589	ERYTHEMATOUS COND NEC	0	0	0	1
6959	ERYTHEMATOUS COND NOS	0	0	0	1

TABLE 4   Diagnoses Used to Identify Adverse Outcomes (Continued)
0 = Not an Adverse Outcome   1 = An Adverse Outcome

ICD-9-CM CODE	Diagnosis	Decubitus	Pneumonia	UTI	Post Op* Infection
6960	PSORIATIC ARTHROPATHY	0	0	0	1
6983	LICHENIFICATION	0	0	0	1
6989	PRURITIC DISORDER NOS	0	0	0	1
7070	DECUBITUS ULCER	1	0	0	0
7718	PERINATAL INFECTION NEC	0	0	0	1
99661	INFEC DUE TO HRT DEVICE	0	0	0	1
99662	INFEC DUE TO VASC DEVICE	0	0	0	1
99663	INFEC DUE TO NERV DEVICE	0	0	0	1
99664	INFECT D/T URETHRAL CATH	0	0	0	1
99665	INFECT D/T GU DEVICE NEC	0	0	0	1
99666	INFEC D/T JOINT PROSTHES	0	0	0	1
99667	INFC D/T ORTH DEVICE NEC	0	0	0	1
99669	INFECT DUE TO DEVICE NEC	0	0	0	1
9985	POSTOPERATIVE INFECTION	0	0	0	1
9993	INFEC COMPL MED CARE NEC	0	0	0	1

*Only applied to surgical patients.

discharges in a DRG. Since the diagnoses flagged as adverse outcomes may or may not have been iatrogenic adverse outcomes, the statewide average adverse outcome rate for a DRG was used as an estimate of the normal rate by which these diagnoses could be expected to occur, and indices were calculated so that hospitals above or below this average (once applied to each hospitals' mix of patient by DRG) were considered to have higher or lower, respectively, adverse outcome rates.

Adverse Outcome Indices

For each DRG, d, in each hospital, h, an expected number of adverse outcomes was calculated for each category of adverse outcome, c, as the statewide adverse outcome rate for the DRG multiplied by the number of discharges (or surgical discharges) in the DRG at that hospital:

Expected Adverse outcomes$_{c,d,h}$ = ($N_{d,h}$ * Statewide adverse outcome rate$_{c,d}$)

Where c = one of the adverse outcome categories,
d = DRG,
h = hospital, and
N = number of discharged patients.

Statewide adverse outcomes rates were used instead of pooling the data from all three states since local coding practice incentives, requirements and other differences could lead to artificial differences in adverse outcome rates across states.

The number of actual and expected adverse outcomes for each category were summed across all DRGs for each hospital. A adverse outcome index for each type of adverse outcome was calculated by hospital as the ratio of actual to expected adverse outcomes:

Adverse outcome Index$_{h,c}$ =

$$\text{Actual adverse outcomes}_{h,c} / \text{Expected adverse outcomes}_{h,c}$$

Length of Stay

Using a similar approach, a relative length of stay index was calculated:

Relative LOS Index$_h$ =

$$\text{Actual geometric mean LOS}_h / \text{Expected geometric mean LOS}_h$$

The actual geometric LOS was calculated by taking the natural logarithm of the LOS for each discharge, summing the logs across all discharges, dividing the sum by the number of discharges, then taking the antilogarithm of the result. Geometric rather than arithmetic means were used because arithmetic means are easily distorted by the presence of even a few unusual cases, or outliers. [An arithmetic mean of N numbers is calculated by adding the N values and dividing the result by N; the corresponding geometric mean is calculated by multiplying the N values and taking the Nth root of the result.] Geometric means provide a stable measure of central tendency without the need to identify and remove specific cases as outliers, and are commonly used in analyses of DRG distributions which typically do not resemble the theoretical bell shaped curve.

$$\text{Actual geometric mean LOS}_h = \exp \left(\sum_{i=1}^{N_h} (\ln(\text{LOS}_{i,h}))/N_h \right)$$

where i = 1, 2, . . N$_h$ discharges in hospital, h,
    ln() is the natural logarithm function,
    exp() is the exponential (antilogarithm) function, and
    LOS$_{i,h}$ is the LOS for patient, i, in hospital, h.

To calculate an expected geometric mean length of stay, the mean log-transformed length of stay for each DRG for the entire state was first calculated:

$$\text{Mean Statewide Log}_d = \left(\sum_{i=1}^{N_d} \ln(\text{LOS}_i) \right)/N_d$$

where i = 1, 2, . N$_d$ discharges in the state in DRG, d.

The expected geometric mean length of stay was then calculated by multiplying the mean statewide log-transformed length of stay for a DRG by the number of discharges at a hospital in that DRG, summing the result across all DRGs, dividing the sum by the number of discharges from the hospital, and taking the antilogarithm of the result:

Expected geometric mean LOS_h =

$$\exp\left(\left(\sum_d (\text{Mean Statewide } LOG_d * N_{d,h})\right)/N_h\right)$$

Hospital Characteristics

Numerous factors in a hospital's environment are likely to impact the incidence of the selected adverse outcomes and patients' lengths of stay. Case-mix is one so basic to nurse staffing and patient outcomes that it was directly adjusted for in expressing the study's staffing, adverse outcome rate and length of stay index variables. Other factors which might intervene may not be satisfactorily measurable from existing data sources, such as the effectiveness of hospitals' environmental service departments. Two variables which are measurable and which have frequently been shown to impact hospitals' costs, staffing and patient outcomes are teaching status and setting (e.g., urban versus rural).

Teaching Status   Teaching hospitals are assumed by some to have more complex cases above and beyond what can be measured using DRGs and NIWs, and this complexity might lead to higher than expected adverse outcome rates. On the other hand, teaching hospitals are the first to receive new techniques in medical and nursing care and products which may reduce adverse outcomes and shorten length of stay compared with non-teaching hospitals. For this study, hospitals were categorized as:

- Medical School Affiliate: A primary undergraduate medical school affiliate (generally one per medical school).
- Other Teaching: Other hospitals with at least 40 residents per 10,000 discharges.
- Non-Teaching: All other hospitals.

Setting   Another factor that can affect adverse outcome rates is the setting—urban vs. rural—in which the hospital operates and draws its patients. For this study, three categories were used:

- Large Urban: Hospitals in Metropolitan Statistical Areas (MSAs) with population over 2,000,000 or in MSAs consolidated into Consolidated Metropolitan Statistical Areas (CMSAs) with populations over 2,000,000.
- Urban: Hospitals in other MSAs.
- Rural: Hospitals not located in an MSA.

Results

Staffing, Adverse Outcomes, Length of Stay and Hospital Characteristics

Table 5 presents NIW acuity, total nurse staffing per day and RN mix (percentage registered nursing of total nursing hours) for California, New York and Massachusetts hospitals, grouped by teaching status and setting. All three states show the same general trends of acuity, staffing levels and skill-mix being greater in those hospitals with the highest degrees of teaching and lowest degrees of urbanity. Between 1992 and 1994, all three states across their levels of teaching and setting showed substantial increases in nurse staffing per patient day and modest increases in registered nurse skill mix and in case-mix acuity. (It should be noted that the NIW method used herein—a single per diem NIW BY DRG—did not measure acuity increases attributable to length of stay compression, although a different method could do so using the input NIW scores developed by the NYSNA panel who scored acuity by day of stay for each DRG. Given the pilot nature of this project, with its first ever statewide applications of NIWs outside of New York, the more conservative single per diem NIW method was tested herein; however the statistical relatedness found between NIWs and actual nursing hours per day would indicate that more advanced NIW applications may be considered in future research).

Table 6 presents the same three nursing structural variables across individual Consolidated Metropolitan Statistical Areas (CMSAs) and Metropolitan Statistical Areas (MSAs) and for each states rural areas combined. Acuity, staffing and RN skill mix were each found to be relatively evenly distributed around the statewide means across geographic settings within each state, with the single standout exception of the New York City CMSA (only including those portions thereof

TABLE 5 Nurse Staffing by Hospital Teachingness and Setting

Hospital Type	Number of Acute Hospitals		Number of Study Hospitals (% Sample)		Avg. NIW Per Day		Avg. Nursing Hours Per Day		Avg. Percent RN	
	1992	1994	1992	1994	1992	1994	1992	1994	1992	1994
A. CALIFORNIA										
All Hospitals	456	463	352 (77%)	295 (64%)	3.54	3.58	7.56	8.43	67.7%	70.5%
Medical School	8	8	8 (100%)	8 (100%)	3.88	3.94	9.33	9.98	79.0%	77.3%
Other Teaching	30	26	26 (87%)	21 (81%)	3.82	3.70	8.62	8.81	76.8%	74.3%
Non-Teaching	418	429	318 (76%)	266 (62%)	3.51	3.56	7.43	8.35	66.6%	70.0%
Large Urban	305	321	241 (79%)	213 (66%)	3.57	3.59	7.42	8.13	71.2%	72.4%
Urban	103	97	81 (79%)	59 (61%)	3.51	3.57	7.71	8.53	61.6%	67.5%
Rural	48	45	30 (63%)	23 (51%)	3.42	3.46	8.25	10.18	55.4%	61.1%
B. NEW YORK										
All Hospitals	232	229	126 (54%)	131 (57%)	3.51	3.56	7.41	8.49	61.0%	62.4%
Medical School	12	15	8 (67%)	11 (73%)	3.60	3.85	9.72	9.84	71.6%	71.3%
Other Teaching	63	62	38 (60%)	28 (45%)	3.49	3.65	6.95	8.10	61.8%	63.8%
Non-Teaching	157	152	80 (51%)	92 (61%)	3.51	3.50	7.40	8.44	59.6%	61.0%
Large Urban	153	112	85 (56%)	64 (57%)	3.52	3.60	7.19	7.50	63.0%	64.1%
Urban	39	72	25 (64%)	44 (61%)	3.52	3.59	8.06	9.55	57.0%	60.6%
Rural	40	45	16 (40%)	23 (51%)	3.45	3.42	7.59	9.19	56.7%	61.6%
C. MASSACHUSETTS										
All Hospitals	95	96	67 (71%)	76 (79%)	3.49	3.56	9.09	9.94	70.3%	71.6%
Medical School	5	5	2 (40%)	3 (60%)	3.81	3.92	9.51	11.51	84.7%	82.9%
Other Teaching	13	14	8 (62%)	12 (86%)	3.64	3.70	10.00	10.83	74.0%	74.9%
Non-Teaching	77	77	57 (74%)	61 (79%)	3.46	3.51	8.90	9.69	69.6%	70.4%
Large Urban	72	73	53 (74%)	61 (84%)	3.50	3.58	8.94	9.94	71.3%	72.1%
Urban	16	16	13 (81%)	14 (88%)	3.47	3.49	9.57	9.85	66.4%	70.0%
Rural	7	7	1 (14%)	1 (14%)	3.39	3.40	10.43	11.61	69.7%	65.8%

located in New York State). The New York metropolitan area's staffing levels were significantly lower in terms of nursing hours per NIW adjusted day than those of upstate New York or Massachusetts MSAs, especially in 1994. This finding is likely related to the extremely long lengths of stay New York City and its suburbs have maintained in recent years, despite sharp declines in nearly all the rest of the nation.

Relationships of Staffing with Patient Outcomes

For the four adverse outcome indicators (pressure ulcers, pneumonia, urinary tract infections, and postoperative infections), and for the length of stay index, regres-

TABLE 6   Nurse Staffing by Hospital Metropolitan Statistical Area

MSA/CMSA	Number		Avg. NIW Per Day		Avg. Nursing Hours Per Day		Avg. Percent RN	
	1992	1994	1992	1994	1992	1994	1992	1994
A. CALIFORNIA								
All Study Hospitals	352	295	3.54	3.58	7.56	8.43	67.7%	70.5%
CMSA:								
Los Angeles	173	144	3.54	3.58	7.37	8.19	69.4%	71.3%
San Diego	19	16	3.62	3.65	7.46	7.95	69.6%	72.2%
San Francisco	60	53	3.59	3.63	7.54	8.02	76.2%	75.4%
MSA:								
Bakersfield	8	6	3.58	3.55	8.75	9.45	48.0%	55.0%
Chico-Paradise	4	3	3.56	3.55	8.88	9.78	49.4%	57.0%
Fresno	10	9	3.54	3.64	7.33	8.75	62.6%	64.2%
Merced	4	3	3.44	3.45	7.50	8.34	52.6%	64.7%
Modesto	4	3	3.61	3.74	7.16	8.45	55.3%	65.6%
Redding	2	2	3.68	3.75	8.12	8.67	76.3%	81.1%
Sacramento	11	9	3.55	3.66	7.26	8.51	69.0%	76.8%
San Luis Obispo	5	5	3.51	3.51	7.29	7.86	78.6%	80.9%
Santa Barbara	6	4	3.49	3.43	8.08	8.60	65.9%	73.7%
Stockton	6	7	3.50	3.55	7.88	8.35	63.0%	66.0%
Visalia	6	3	3.42	3.48	7.69	9.66	48.9%	59.8%
Yolo	2	3	3.42	3.42	8.47	11.40	77.9%	71.5%
Yuba City	2	2	3.51	3.53	7.56	8.21	44.3%	53.5%
rural	30	23	3.42	3.46	8.25	10.18	55.4%	61.1%
B. NEW YORK								
All Study Hospitals	126	131	3.51	3.56	7.41	8.49	61.0%	62.4%
CMSA:								
New York	69	64	3.51	3.60	6.99	7.50	63.8%	64.1%
MSA:								
Albany/Troy/Schenectady	5	6	3.58	3.66	7.77	9.83	72.4%	70.4%
Binghamton	0	2	–	3.54	–	8.45	–	70.0%
Buffalo/Niagara Falls	15	16	3.54	3.60	7.85	8.74	58.5%	57.6%
Elmira	1	1	3.44	3.82	9.35	11.63	70.7%	75.1%
Glens Falls	1	2	3.57	3.53	9.14	10.47	61.0%	47.7%
Jamestown	3	3	3.43	3.40	9.77	10.61	50.5%	56.7%
Rochester	7	6	3.49	3.53	7.83	10.22	53.5%	63.5%
Syracuse	6	5	3.58	3.62	8.31	9.45	51.5%	58.0
Utica	3	4	3.52	3.63	6.96	10.64	57.6%	57.5%
rural	16	22	3.45	3.41	7.59	9.11	56.7%	61.7%
C. MASSACHUSETTS								
All Study Hospitals	67	76	3.49	3.56	9.09	9.94	70.3%	71.6%
MSA:								
Barnstable	2	2	3.34	3.47	10.60	9.54	60.7%	74.0%
Boston/Worcester/Lowell/ Lawrence/Brockton	53	61	3.50	3.58	8.94	9.54	71.3%	72.1%
Pittsfield	4	4	3.46	3.44	9.45	10.55	68.7%	67.8%
Springfield	7	8	3.51	3.53	9.34	9.57	66.8%	70.1%
rural	1	1	3.39	3.40	10.43	11.61	69.7%	65.8%

TABLE 7   Significance Levels Correlations of Dependent Variables with One or More Independent Variables

State	Year	Geo. LOS Index		Decubitus		Pneum		Postop. Inf.		UTI	
		Sig. Level	R²	Sig. Level	R²	Sig. Level	R²	Sig. Level	R²	Sig. Level	R²
MASS.	1992	p < .01	28.9%	P < .05	7.1%	not sig.	–	not sig.	–	not sig.	–
MASS.	1994	p < .05	6.2%	not sig.	–	p < .05	6.3%	not sig.	–	not sig.	–
N.Y.	1992	p < .01	36.0%	p < .01	15.0%	p < .01	10.6%	p < .05	3.9%	p < .01	14.0%
N.Y.	1994	p < .01	26.1%	p < .01	11.1%	p < .01	8.1%	p < .05	3.6%	p < .01	6.9%
CALIF.	1992	p < .01	14.8%	p < .01	14.7%	p < .01	14.1%	p < .01	0.2%	p < .01	12.9%
CALIF.	1994	p < .01	14.4%	p < .01	14.1%	p < .01	11.2%	p < .05	3.3%	p < .01	8.5%

sions were performed individually for New York, California, and Massachusetts for 1992 and 1994 respectively, to test their relationship with the study's independent variables: teaching status, setting, total nursing hours per NIW and registered nurse percentage of total nursing hours.

As shown in Table 7 above, statistically significant relationships were found for each of the dependent variables (the four adverse outcome rates and the geometric length of stay index) for New York and California hospitals in both 1992 and 1994. Statistically significant relationships were also found for the geometric length of stay of Massachusetts hospitals in 1992 and 1994. However, in 1992, only decubitus rates were found to be related statistically to any of the independent variables for Massachusetts, and in 1994, only pneumonia was statistically significant. Because statistical relationships were found for all four adverse outcome rates in both years for New York and California but only once for Massachusetts, it can reasonably be surmised that there may be a lack of complete and accurate collection and/or submission of diagnosis information on the part of Massachusetts hospitals to the Massachusetts Rate Setting Commission. On the other hand, in all six cases (the three states for both years) the geometric length of stay index was statistically related to independent variables, leading to the conclusion that this information has been accurately collected by Massachusetts hospitals. It should be noted that the degree of coding effort needed for DRG payment optimization is probably not sufficient for reporting specific secondary adverse outcomes used in the analyses herein.

Table 8 displays the coefficients of the six independent variables for all equations in which the geometric length of stay index was the dependent variable and the relationship was significant. For example, in New York in 1994, all other variables being held constant, an increase of one hour of nursing care per NIW would predict a geometric length of stay in a hospital 4.4% lower than the average for the state; a ten percent increase in the mix of registered nurses relative to other skill levels of nurses would predict a geometric length of stay .11% lower than the average; and being a rural hospital predicted a 3.9% lower geometric length of stay. The point that stands out most prominently from this set of regressions is

TABLE 8   **Geometric Length of Stay Index**

State	Year	Total Hours Per NIW	Percent RN Hours	Medical School	Other Teaching	Large Urban	Rural
				Independent Variables			
MASS.	1992	−9.70%	−0.27%	not sig.	not sig.	not sig.	not sig.
MASS.	1994	not sig.	−0.19%	not sig.	not sig.	not sig.	not sig.
N.Y.	1992	−6.46%	−0.19%	not sig.	+5.40%	+9.22%	not sig.
N.Y.	1994	−4.40%	−0.11%	not sig.	not sig.	not sig.	−3.94%
CALIF.	1992	−4.82%	−0.07%	not sig.	+7.15%	not sig.	−6.48%
CALIF.	1994	−5.40%	−0.16%	not sig.	9.55%	not sig.	not sig.

TABLE 9   **Pressure Ulcer Adverse Outcome Rates**

State	Year	Total Hours Per NIW	Percent RN Hours	Medical School	Teaching	Large Urban	Rural
N.Y.	1992	−17.89%	−1.77%	not sig.	not sig.	+28.10%	not sig.
N.Y.	1994	not sig.	−1.23%	not sig.	not sig.	+24.29%	not sig.
CALIF.	1992	not sig.	−0.79%	not sig.	−37.92%	+41.39%	not sig.
CALIF.	1994	−15.59%	−1.23%	not sig.	−35.23%	+38.51%	not sig.

that more nursing hours per NIW and a higher skill mix of nurses are associated with reduced hospital lengths of stay. In five of six cases, total hours per NIW were significantly and inversely related to length of stay, and in all six cases , the RN percentage of total nursing hours was significantly and inversely related to length of stay. It was also found in two instances that rural hospitals (New York in 1994 and California in 1992) tend to have shorter lengths of stay. Additionally - and not surprisingly - teaching hospitals overall (New York in 1992, California in 1992 and 1994) and large urban hospitals (New York in 1992) have longer lengths of stay. Whether or not a hospital is a primary medical school affiliate does not have any clear statistical relationship with length of stay.

The following discussion of pressure ulcer rates, pneumonia rates, postoperative infection rates and urinary tract infection rates (and the accompanying tables) exclude Massachusetts because of the aforementioned issues with data quality and lack of statistically significant relationships and will focus only on New York and California for 1992 and 1994.

Several factors were related to pressure ulcer rates in New York and California in 1992 and 1994 (See Table 9 above). The level of nurse staffing would seem to play a role in a hospitals' pressure ulcer rates. In two of the four cases (New York in 1992 and California in 1994) additional hours of nursing per NIW were related to lower rates of pressure ulcers. Further, in all four cases, nursing skill mix is related to pressure ulcer rates. Each additional percent of nursing personnel that were registered nurses was associated with a reduction in the pressure ulcer rate by between three-fourths and one and three-fourths percent in these cases.

Table 9 also shows that if a New York hospital was located in a large urban area (i.e., New York City CMSA) it had on average (all else being equal) pressure ulcer rates more than twenty-four percent higher than the average hospital. California hospitals located in large urban settings had pressure ulcer rates forty-one percent higher (1992) or thirty-eight percent higher (1994) than hospitals located in areas with fewer than two million persons. Teaching hospitals in California, on the other hand, were found to have a more than thirty-five percent lower pressure ulcer rate than other teaching hospitals, all else being equal. In all four cases, neither medical school affiliate hospitals nor rural hospitals had any statistically significant differences in pressure ulcer rates than other hospitals located in their states, again with all else being equal.

The relationship between the independent variables and pneumonia rates is less clearly defined than was the case for pressure ulcer rates (See Table 10). Each of the independent variables except rural location was statistically significantly related to pneumonia rates in at least one of the four cases, but only RN skill mix and large urban location were statistically significant in at least two of the four cases. As with pressure ulcers, when there was a statistically significant relationship, a higher mix of registered nurses was associated with lower rates of pneumonia adverse outcomes. If a hospital was a primary medical school affiliate (New York in 1992) or other teaching facility (New York in 1994), pneumonia rates were found to be lower by more than fifteen percent. Perhaps the most interesting finding in regard to pneumonia rates was that large urban hospitals had lower rates than hospitals located in smaller areas, all else being equal. Although further study is necessary to determine the reasons for lower pneumonia rates in large urban hospitals, it is true that most of the hospitals situated in large urban areas in New York and California are located close to sea level in proximity to large bodies of water and in more temperate areas where the air contains more moisture. Less populated areas of these states tend to be colder and drier, sometimes in more mountainous territory where the air is thinner. Hospitals located in these latter areas also tend to be smaller with more erratic and lower occupancies and hence higher nurse staffing levels. A positive relationship between nurse staffing and pneumonia adverse outcomes rates was found to be driven by a relatively small number of hospitals in high desert areas and the Sierra Nevada with both high staffing levels and pneumonia adverse outcome rates.

TABLE 10   Pneumonia Rates

State	Year	Total Hours Per NIW	Percent RN Hours	Medical School	Teaching	Large Urban	Rural
N.Y.	1992	not sig.	not sig.	−18.24%	not sig.	−11.62%	not sig
N.Y.	1994	not sig.	not sig.	not sig.	−15.80%	not sig.	not sig.
CALIF.	1992	not sig.	−0.56%	not sig.	not sig.	−9.14%	not sig.
CALIF.	1994	+7.65%*	−0.39%	not sig.	not sig.	−9.54%	not sig.

*When seven hospitals located in high mountain or desert areas are excluded, this variable is no longer statistically significant.

TABLE 11   Postoperative Infection Rates

State	Year	Total Hours Per NIW	Percent RN Hours	Medical School	Teaching	Large Urban	Rural
N.Y.	1992	not sig.	not sig.	not sig.	not sig.	not sig.	− 12.18%
N.Y.	1994	not sig.	not sig.	not sig.	not sig.	+ 7.84%	not sig.
CALIF.	1992	not sig.	− 0.53%	not sig.	not sig.	not sig.	− 19.03%
CALIF.	1994	not sig.	− 0.47%	not sig.	not sig.	+ 9.65%	not sig.

TABLE 12   Urinary Tract Infection Adverse Outcome Rates

State	Year	Total Hours Per NIW	Percent RN Hours	Medical School	Teaching	Large Urban	Rural
N.Y.	1992	not sig.	not sig.	not sig.	− 12.17%	not sig.	− 28.54%
N.Y.	1994	not sig.	− 0.65%	not sig.	not sig.	not sig.	not sig.
CALIF.	1992	not sig.	− 0.64%	not sig.	− 23.01%	+ 9.79%	− 24.14%
CALIF.	1994	not sig.	− 0.65%	not sig.	− 19.75%	not sig.	− 22.84%

Regressions to test the relationship of the independent variables to postoperative infection rates showed once again that in two of the four cases, nursing skill mix is statistically and inversely related to postoperative infection rates (See Table 11). For both years in California, more registered nurses as a percentage of all nurse staffing were associated with lower postoperative infection rates, although this relationship was not found to be statistically significant in either year in New York.

The setting of a hospital was also found to be related to postoperative infection rates in the two states. In 1992, if a hospital in either state was located in a rural area, it was likely to have a rate more than twelve percent (New York) or nineteen percent (California) lower than a hospital in a non-rural area. In 1994, hospitals located in a large urban area MSA were found to have postoperative infection rates more than seven percent higher (New York) or nine percent higher (California) than the average rate for all hospitals in each state respectively. Being affiliated with a medical school or otherwise being a teaching hospital, and the total number of nursing hours per NIW were not statistically related to postoperative infection rates in any of the four cases.

Table 12 shows the relationship between the independent variables and urinary tract infection adverse outcome rates for New York and California hospitals for 1992 and 1994. In three of the four cases, a statistically significant relationship existed between nursing skill mix and urinary tract infection rates. In New York (1994) and California (1992 and 1994), each additional percentage of registered nurses was associated with a nearly two-thirds of one percent lower UTI rate. The total number of nursing hours per NIW was not statistically related to the UTI rate in any of the cases.

A hospital's affiliation with a medical school also was not statistically related to a hospital's UTI rate (all four cases). However, if a hospital had a teaching affiliation, it had a lower urinary tract infection rate by more than twelve percent (New York in 1992) or more than nineteen (California in 1992) or twenty-three percent (California in 1994). Finally, the setting of a hospital was also associated with its UTI adverse outcome rate. In one of four cases, California in 1992, hospitals located in large urban areas were likely to have higher UTI rates than non-large urban area hospitals by more than nine percent, and in three of four cases, rural hospitals had UTI adverse outcome rates more than twenty percent lower than non-rural hospitals. The incidence of urinary catheterization rates may be similarly lower in rural areas, potentially accounting for this finding.

Discussion

This project was able to successfully achieve several of its goals and objectives:

■ Several of the process and outcome indicators proposed for the Nursing Report Card for Acute Care Settings were quantitatively expressed and measured for several hundred hospitals across three states for two different years;

■ Shorter lengths of stay were found to be strongly statistically related to higher nurse staffing per acuity adjusted day;

■ Patient morbidity indicators for preventable conditions often arising as a result of hospitalization—pressure ulcers, pneumonia, postoperative infections and urinary tract infections—were found to be statistically significantly related with lower registered nurse skill mixes and, to a lesser extent, less nurse staffing per acuity adjusted day; and

■ Nursing Intensity Weights by DRG, a methodology developed by New York State in order to measure patient acuity and nursing workload attributable to diagnostically related case-mix differences, were found to be statistically significantly related to differences in nurse staffing ratios per patient day in all three states.

However, the project was not conducted without difficulties. Chief among these were the data quality (and timeliness) problems encountered with the state data sets. In each of the three states, a large proportion of hospitals had to be excluded from the study due to non-reporting or obviously errant reporting of certain data items, especially nursing hours. Secondly, the reporting of complicating secondary diagnoses—especially those which may have been iatrogenically induced—was likely significantly lacking for Massachusetts hospitals, and probably to a lesser extent in the other states as well. Hospitals' natural inclinations will always be to under report such conditions relative to all other diagnoses, especially if payments are not directly involved. While this study's approach would seem to yield fruitful results for the nursing profession, it is recommended that its data sources be circumspected to determine whether Federal sources may be substituted, albeit at the cost of losing non-federal patients for some (but not all) purposes.

With cleaner input data and better standardized reporting, the likelihood will be even greater that strong relationships between more nursing and shorter lengths of stay and lower rates of morbidity will be found.